ROMANS

FROM BROKEN TO BELONGING

NOE GARCIA

Lifeway Press®
Nashville, Tennessee

Editorial Team

Reid Patton
Writer

Jennifer Siao
Production Editor

Brett McIntosh
Content Editor

Jon Rodda
Art Director

Joel Polk
Editorial Team Leader

Brian Daniel
Manager and Publisher, Adult Ministry

Ben Mandrell
President, Lifeway Christian Resources

Published by Lifeway Press® • © 2021 Noe Garcia

No part of this book may be reproduced or transmitted in any form or by any means, electronic or mechanical, including photocopying and recording, or by any information storage or retrieval system, except as may be expressly permitted in writing by the publisher. Requests for permission should be addressed in writing to Lifeway Press®; One Lifeway Plaza; Nashville, TN 37234.

ISBN 978-1-0877-4823-8 • Item 005833481

Dewey decimal classification: 227.1
Subject heading: BIBLE / New Testament / Romans 8 / Study and Teaching / Pain / Suffering

Unless otherwise noted, Scripture quotations are taken from the ESV® Bible (The Holy Bible, English Standard Version®), copyright © 2001 by Crossway, a publishing ministry of Good News Publishers. Used by permission. All rights reserved.

To order additional copies of this resource, write to Lifeway Resources Customer Service; One Lifeway Plaza; Nashville, TN 37234; fax 615-251-5933; phone toll free 800-458-2772; order online at Lifeway.com; or email orderentry@lifeway.com.

Printed in the United States of America

Adult Ministry Publishing • Lifeway Resources
One Lifeway Plaza • Nashville, TN 37234

CONTENTS

ABOUT THE AUTHOR

Noe Garcia began his spiritual journey at age 18 and surrendered fully to God's will for his life. He became the Senior Pastor at North Phoenix in 2016. Noe is a passionate preacher who loves challenging and encouraging people with God's Word.

Pastor Noe holds a Doctor of Ministry in Executive Leadership from Southern Baptist Theological Seminary, Masters of Divinity from Golden Gate Baptist Theological Seminary and a Bachelors of Kinesiology with a minor in Religion from East Texas Baptist University.

In addition to being a Senior Pastor, Noe also serves as an Adjunct Professor for Gateway Seminary, Board of Trustees member for Union University, an Ethics and Religious Liberty Commission Leadership Council member, and a member of the Evangelism Young Leaders Committees North American Mission Board.

HOW TO USE THIS STUDY

Romans 8: From Brokenness to Belonging provides a guided process for individuals and small groups to walk through the eighth chapter of Romans. This Bible study book includes eight sessions of content, each divided into two major sections: "Group Study" and "Personal Study." A leader guide is also provided to prepare those who are leading groups through this journey.

GROUP STUDY

Regardless of the day of the week your group meets, each week of content begins with a group session. This group session is designed to last sixty minutes, with approximately ten minutes dedicated to video teaching and another forty-five minutes to group discussion and prayer. Meeting even longer than sixty minutes will allow more time for participants to interact with one another.

Each group study uses the following format to facilitate simple yet meaningful interaction among group members, with God's Word, and with the video teaching.

START
This section includes questions to get the conversation started, a review of the previous week's study to reinforce the content, and an introduction to the new content for the current week.

WATCH
This section provides space for taking notes as participants watch the video. Codes to access the teaching videos included with your purchase of this book can be found on the insert located at the back of this book.

DISCUSS

This section includes discussion questions that guide the group to respond to the video teaching and to relevant Bible passages. This section includes plenty of space to take notes during the group session

PERSONAL STUDY

In addition to the group study, each session includes three personal study sections to further explore and reinforce the biblical teaching from the group time. Each personal study features the following three sections.

READ

This section expands the teaching on the text of Scripture explored in the group study through practical Bible study activities, commentary, and reflective questions. The read section leads individuals to understanding and further discovery.

REFLECT

This section guides participants to reflect upon, digest, and apply the biblical truths covered in the week's session. This short section covers two pages and gives participants time and space to adjust their hearts and minds in response to God's Word.

REHEARSE

One of the best ways to apply God's Word to our lives is to hide it in our hearts. The rehearse section guides participants to memorize Romans 8:31-39 over the course of the 8-session study. Each rehearse section includes practical memorization tips as well as space to write out the verses each week. Additionally, Scripture memory cards are located in the back of the study.

ROMANS 8

FROM BROKEN TO BELONGING

SESSION 1

Shame

GROUP STUDY

Start

Welcome everyone to session 1.

What is a movie or show you would watch over and over again without getting tired of it?

Many scholars and pastors have called Romans 8 the greatest chapter in all the Bible. At first this may seem like a bold claim or even heretical—after all, the whole Bible is equally inspired by the Spirit of God, right? What they mean is that Romans 8 is filled with so many essential truths that it merits deep study and repeated reflection. So over the next 8 sessions, we're going to dig into Romans 8 a few verses at a time. Together, we'll see why generations of Christians have returned to this chapter again and again.

What are your hopes for studying during these next 8 weeks?

To prepare for video session 1, pray that God will help each person understand and apply this truth:

Jesus frees us from sin and condemnation.

To access the teaching sessions, use the instructions in the back of your Bible study book.

Watch

*Use the space below to take notes while
you watch video session 1.*

Discuss

*Use the following questions to guide
your discussion of the video.*

Begin by reading Romans 8:1-4 together.

1. Romans 8:1 offers extraordinary hope to ordinary sinners. How is this verse challenging, encouraging, or convicting to you?

2. In this session, Noe described the shame he used to deal with as paralyzing. Shame can be more than a feeling. What are some ways shame can affect us mentally, physically, and emotionally?

3. Noe also said, "Shame has you running when no one is chasing or hiding, when no one is looking." How does shame harm our relationship with God and other people?

4. Read Psalm 32:3-5. What happened to David when he kept his sin to himself? What happened when he confessed? How does God respond to our sin differently than we do?

5. What has been your experience when you've tried to cover or hide your sin from God or other people? Why are our attempts to run and hide from sin never helpful?

6. How does acknowledging and confessing our sin empty shame of its power? What keeps us from confessing our sins to one another? What are we afraid will happen if we're honest about our shame and struggles?

7. We have a God who wants to cover our sins and embrace us. How does the gospel give us all the power to come out from hiding?

8. What are ways we can encourage one another to become free from shame and embrace the richness and power of the gospel?

Remind group members to complete this session's personal study, then close your time together in prayer thanking God for freeing us from shame and condemnation.

READ

Romans 8 is a trinitarian passage. From the beginning of the chapter we see all three persons of the Trinity—God the Father, God the Son, and God the Holy Spirit—working together to bring life and freedom to the Christian.

As you read the following verses, circle every reference to God, Jesus, and the Holy Spirit. List the actions of each in the space below.

¹ There is therefore now no condemnation for those who are in Christ Jesus. ² For the law of the Spirit of life has set you free in Christ Jesus from the law of sin and death. ³ For God has done what the law, weakened by the flesh, could not do. By sending his own Son in the likeness of sinful flesh and for sin, he condemned sin in the flesh, ⁴ in order that the righteous requirement of the law might be fulfilled in us, who walk not according to the flesh but according to the Spirit.
ROMANS 8:1-4

God the Father:

God the Son:

God the Holy Spirit:

Summarize the main point of these verses in your own words.

The incredible truth at the center of these verses and the center of the gospel itself is that there is no condemnation for those who have placed their faith in Jesus. Father, Son, and Spirit have worked together to ensure that anyone who comes to Jesus can be forever free from the penalty of sin. In Christ, we are free. The Father ordered it, the Son fulfilled it, and the Spirit confirms it.

What does it mean to be condemned? When do you feel condemned?

Why is it so easy for us to feel condemned even though we know Christ has redeemed us from our sins?

The word *condemnation* is a legal term. We go before the judge. The judge bangs his gavel and gives us the sentence. But for the believer, God has looked at our resumé of sins—all the times we've broken His law—and just as He's about to judge us, Jesus steps in and says, "No, I'll take their punishment. If they will believe in me, I will take their life sentence for them." Instead of a life sentence apart from God, we've been given life and freedom with God. Because of Christ's sacrifice, the Holy Spirit has taken residency in us, which has freed us from the eternal consequences of sin. Not because we've done anything, but because of what Jesus has done for us. Yet despite all of this, some of us live as though we're still condemned.

When has your sin left you feeling guilt-ridden, trapped, or ashamed? How did you respond to those feelings?

Despite the freedom we've received in Christ, we often feel trapped. We are burdened by worry and the weight of our sins. When we cling to the burden, we lose sight of the freedom God gives us through Christ. We believe what shame says about us more than what God says about us. It's a cycle that's hard to defeat. The great news is that even in our weakness and failure to believe, God has still forgiven us and washed us. Our lack of believing in our own forgiveness doesn't make us any less forgiven.

Look back over Romans 8:1-4 and identify what God done to free us from condemnation?

Verse 1

Verse 2

Verse 3

Verse 4

Based on the promises you identified, how should you respond the next time you feel condemned by your sin and guilt?

You don't have to beat yourself up for the things you did five days ago, or five minutes ago. Remember the benefits of being in Christ. You're not condemned (v. 1), you're set free (v. 2), God's righteousness is given to you in Christ (v. 3), and you now have the power to walk in freedom through the Spirit of God (v. 4). Your sin is not your identity, the work of Christ is! You have been given the power to deny your flesh and walk in the Spirit.

What confidence should it give you to know that God has done everything necessary for you to live free from shame and condemnation?

Many Christians have been set free but live as if they are still accused and condemned. If you are a person who is shame and guilt-ridden, let me encourage you. Let it go! Leave the cuffs in the courtroom. You are no longer tied to your crime, and you do not have to pay the time. No condemnation means no more carrying the punishment and consequences that breed shame!

> *Thank God for the freedom He's given you in Christ.*
> *Lay aside your shame and embrace His forgiveness.*

REFLECT

If you find yourself wrestling with shame over sin, the Scriptures provide a pathway to experiencing the condemnation-free life Romans 8 speaks about.

If we confess our sins, he is faithful and just to forgive us our sins and to cleanse us from all unrighteousness.
1 JOHN 1:9

Instead of allowing your sin to drive you to shame, acknowledge it, confess it, and be forgiven! Acknowledge the very thing that is producing that shame. Get a journal and confess it to the Lord. He can handle whatever you have to bring to Him. And if makes it any easier for you, He already knows about it. I promise you, there is freedom and rest on the other side of this.

Where do you feel condemned? Acknowledge those areas.

What sins do you need to confess?

What has God done to free you from those sins? How will you accept and embrace His forgiveness?

In addition to writing and confessing these areas to God, I would also encourage you to find a trusted friend.

Who is a trusted friend you can share these things with?

REHEARSE

One of the best ways to rehearse God's truths in our lives is to memorize Scripture. Over these 8 sessions, we will memorize the last 9 verses of Romans 8.

What then shall we say to these things?
If God is for us, who can be against us?
ROMANS 8:31

Start by reading this verse slowly ten times (yes, ten times). Next, use the space provided to write it out several times. Try to read over this verse a few times a day to build your memory.

A Scripture memory card for this verse can be found on p. 139.

ROMANS

8

FROM BROKEN TO BELONGING

SESSION 2

Battlefield

GROUP STUDY

Start

Welcome everyone to session 2.

**Are you a glass half-full or glass half-empty person?
Give an example.**

Last session, we looked at the cornerstone truth that every believer is free from condemnation because of the work of God—Father, Son, and Spirit— in his or her life. However, even though we're saved and secure in Christ, it's often hard to let go of lingering feelings of shame and condemnation. In this session, we're going to take a closer look at where those feelings come from. We're going to look at the battle that's playing out in our minds between the Spirit and the flesh.

When have you felt the tension between your freedom in Christ and the struggles of the moment?

To prepare for video session 2, pray that God will help each person understand and apply this truth:

> Setting your mind on the cross helps you embrace the Spirit's work in your life.

To access the teaching sessions, use the instructions in the back of your Bible study book.

Watch

*Use the space below to take notes while
you watch video session 2.*

Discuss

*Use the following questions to guide
your discussion of the video.*

Begin by reading Romans 8:5-11 together.

1. Noe began by saying, "What we believe will control how we behave."
   How have you found this to be true?

2. Why do we hide our spiritual battles from one another? How could people
   in this group actually support one another when dealing with the kind of
   hardships Noe described in this teaching?

3. Have you ever tried to bargain with God to remove a hardship from you?
   Why might this be unhelpful? How do we learn to trust God even when life
   isn't going well for us?

4. The devil wants us to take our minds off the cross and focus them on our
   flesh. How do we make that easy for him? What are the things that take our
   minds off of the cross and off of truth and pull them to other things?

5. Noe mentioned that we can win the battle of our minds by memorizing
   Scripture and telling ourselves truth over and over again. Did you begin
   memorizing Romans 8:31 last week? How did that go?

6. Other than Scripture memory, what are some other spiritual practices that can help us walk in confidence against the attacks we face? How can we help each other in these things?

7. Read 2 Corinthians 10:3-5. How can we practice the truth of this verse together? How can we recenter each other on the truth?

As you end your time together, remind group members to complete this session's personal study, then pray and ask the Spirit to help you set your minds on Him and the work He's doing in your lives.

READ

The part of Romans 8 we're studying in this session is about two states of mind or ways of life that exist in opposition to one another—the way of the Spirit and the way of the flesh. One produces life and the other produces life and peace.

As you read the following passage, underline every time you see the words "mind," "flesh," or "Spirit."

> *⁵ For those who live according to the flesh set their minds on the things of the flesh, but those who live according to the Spirit set their minds on the things of the Spirit. ⁶ For to set the mind on the flesh is death, but to set the mind on the Spirit is life and peace. ⁷ For the mind that is set on the flesh is hostile to God, for it does not submit to God's law; indeed, it cannot. ⁸ Those who are in the flesh cannot please God.*
> *⁹ You, however, are not in the flesh but in the Spirit, if in fact the Spirit of God dwells in you. Anyone who does not have the Spirit of Christ does not belong to him. ¹⁰ But if Christ is in you, although the body is dead because of sin, the Spirit is life because of righteousness. ¹¹ If the Spirit of him who raised Jesus from the dead dwells in you, he who raised Christ Jesus from the dead will also give life to your mortal bodies through his Spirit who dwells in you.*
> ROMANS 8:5-11

According to this passage, how do our thoughts determine the way we live?

In the columns below, list how Paul described the way of the flesh and the way of the Spirit.

FLESH	SPIRIT

Hopefully you see the contrast Paul made. Examine it a little more closely beginning with the mind set on the flesh. In the original context, Paul was contrasting believers, and unbelievers, but we would be foolish to ignore that even the most mature Christians occasionally set their minds of the flesh. *Set their minds* means to be absorbed or focused on something. A mind set on the flesh produces a life that leaves brokenness everywhere it goes.

Read Galatians 5:16-21. How else did Paul describe people with their minds set on the flesh?

When have you embraced the kind of fleshly habits Paul described in Romans 8 and Galatians 5?

What must happen for a Christian to deny his or her flesh and live according to the Spirit?

The Christian life is a struggle with sin, not a surrender to sin. There's a big difference. The Christian struggles with sin. The one who is not a Christian is surrendered to sin. This side of heaven, we will never be able to cease sinning altogether, but a fleshly mindset shouldn't become our standard way of living. Sure, we will struggle, but there is a way to live in victory now. We must live according to the Spirit.

Refer to Galatians 5:22-25. What does it look like when a Christian walks according to the Spirit?

Christians don't come to Jesus fully formed; we must grow in our ability to depend on the Spirit. Through the process of sanctification, we become more dependent on Jesus and less dependent on our flesh. Unfortunately, our flesh doesn't go away. We all still have struggles. But, there is a way to live in victory now—to set our minds, to be absorbed in the life giving Spirit of God. You win the battle of your mind by fighting the lies of your flesh with truth from the Spirit.

As Christians, we have several weapons available to us to deny our flesh and walk in the Spirit. How do each of the following help us set our minds on the Spirit?

Prayer:

Community:

The truth of God's Word:

Christians must set our minds on the things of the Spirit because those things are what bring life and peace. Your reality remains true, but the difference is you now see with a new perspective. You see your sin and know you are forgiven. You can take traumatic experiences and know that what the enemy intended for harm, God can use for good (Gen. 50:20). You no longer look at your life through the lens of condemnation and destruction, but instead, you look through the lens of life and peace.

> *Thank God for the Spirit at work in your life. Ask God to lead you into the kind of life and peace that only comes from the Spirit.*

REFLECT

The mind is a powerful battlefield. If you are anything like me, then truth struggles to stay alive. Truthful thoughts have a short lifespan. Lies, on the other hand, have learned to set up post and become long faithful residents. The battle is between thinking thoughts that are good, true, and noble or giving in to those that are self-deprecating and untruthful. It's hand-to-hand combat between truths and lies. It's a battle we will all face and a battle we must be prepared to fight

Read and meditate on the following Scriptures about where we set our minds, then answer the questions on the following page.

³ For though we walk in the flesh, we are not waging war according to the flesh. ⁴ For the weapons of our warfare are not of the flesh but have divine power to destroy strongholds. ⁵ We destroy arguments and every lofty opinion raised against the knowledge of God, and take every thought captive to obey Christ.
2 CORINTHIANS 10:3-5

¹ I appeal to you therefore, brothers, by the mercies of God, to present your bodies as a living sacrifice, holy and acceptable to God, which is your spiritual worship. ² Do not be conformed to this world, but be transformed by the renewal of your mind, that by testing you may discern what is the will of God, what is good and acceptable and perfect.
ROMANS 12:1-2

Finally, brothers, whatever is true, whatever is honorable,
Whatever is just, whatever is pure, whatever is lovely,
whatever is commendable, if there is any excellence, if there
is anything worthy of praise, think about these things.
PHILIPPIANS 4:8

What are some lies you are believing? How are these lies affecting your spiritual health?

What are some truths you are learning from the Spirit of God at work in your life?

What do you need to change about the way you think in light of the truth from God's Word?

REHEARSE

One of the best ways to rehearse God's truths in our lives is to memorize Scripture. Last session we began with Romans 8:31. This week we continue with verse 32. If you didn't start last session, try picking it up this week. Setting your mind on God's Word is always rewarding.

He who did not spare his own Son but
gave him up for us all, how will he not also
with him graciously give us all things?
ROMANS 8:32

Begin this week by rereading Romans 8:31 to refresh your memory. Then read this week's verse 10 times slowly. As you grow more comfortable, read them together. Use the blank space to write out the verses a few times.

A Scripture memory card for this verse can be found on page 139.

....

....

....

....

....

....

....

....

....

ROMANS

FROM BROKEN TO BELONGING

8

SESSION 3

Philophobia

GROUP STUDY

Start

Welcome everyone to session 3.

Last session, we talked about how we need to tell ourselves the truths of Scripture over and over again. How does memorizing Scripture aid in this process?

This session is all about what happens when we are afraid to love or receive love. What are some reasons someone might be afraid of being loved?

Philophobia is the fear of love or being loved (*philo* meaning love; *phobia* meaning fear). At first this might seem like a silly or uncommon fear, but it affects more people than you may realize. Recall all those times you felt like you weren't enough or that you lacked something essential. These are all instances of philophobia. What's more, we often take these fears into our relationship with God. For the Christian, this fear is completely unfounded. In this session, we will see how all Christians are loved and accepted by God as beloved children.

To prepare for video session 3, pray that God will help each person understand and apply this truth:

God loves you.

To access the teaching sessions, use the instructions in the back of your Bible study book.

Watch

*Use the space below to take notes while
you watch video session 3.*

Discuss

*Use the following questions to guide
your discussion of the video.*

Begin by reading Romans 8:12-17 together.

1. Noe shared how he once asked God to show him a shooting star as a sign
    of His love. Why do we crave signs from God? Why is it always better to
    consult God's Word rather than request signs when we're distressed?

2. Look at Romans 8:15. Even after we've become Christians, why do we allow
    bad choices or questionable decisions from our pasts lead us to fall back
    into a spirit of fear and slavery? What are some ways we can reassure one
    another of God's love for us?

3. All Christians have been given a Spirit of adoption. The first benefit of
    adoption is that our debt has been removed. How does forgiveness allow
    us to live with the love and freedom God intended?

4. Adoption also gives us a new name; we belong to God. What does the idea
    of adoption teach us about what it means to be a child of God? How should
    our adoption affect the way we live? What about the way we relate to one
    another?

5. Our adoption made us heirs with Christ. What resources do we inherit as
    God's children? Why do we approach God as if His resources could run out?

6. Which aspect of adoption do you most need to embrace? Which is the hardest for you to embrace? How can we help each other embrace our adoption?

7. Adoption is a beautiful picture of the gospel at work in our lives. How could you use these verses and the idea of adoption to share the gospel with an unbelieving friend?

As you end your time together, thank God for adopting you into His family. Thank Him for all the benefits that come from being His children, then remind group members to complete this session's personal study.

READ

These verses are all about how the Holy Spirit works in the life of a believer. He guides you out of the spirit of slavery to sin and into a spirit of adoption.

As you read the following passage, underline every instance of the Spirit. Take notice where the word is capitalized—signifying the Holy Spirit.

12 So then, brothers, we are debtors, not to the flesh, to live according to the flesh. 13 For if you live according to the flesh you will die, but if by the Spirit you put to death the deeds of the body, you will live. 14 For all who are led by the Spirit of God are sons of God. 15 For you did not receive the spirit of slavery to fall back into fear, but you have received the Spirit of adoption as sons, by whom we cry, "Abba! Father!" 16 The Spirit himself bears witness with our spirit that we are children of God, 17 and if children, then heirs—heirs of God and fellow heirs with Christ, provided we suffer with him in order that we may also be glorified with him.
ROMANS 8:12-17

Based on these verses, list the ways the Holy Spirit is at work in the life of every believer.

Continuing through Romans 8, Paul taught that the Holy Spirit keeps us from falling back into slavery to sin and flesh, and He allows us to cry out to God as Father. He bears witness that we are children of God, and He helps us see our inheritance in Christ. Let's take a closer look at each of these benefits.

How does the Holy Spirit support us in our fight against sin?

What would be different about your struggle against sin if you relied on the leadership of the Holy Spirit?

What is the role of the Holy Spirit to help us fight against our fear of being loved?

The greatest leaders are good followers, and when the Spirit comes in, we no longer live without a leader. Before we were spiritual orphans, held captive to the desires of our flesh. The Spirit arrives at the moment of salvation and never departs. On the cross, there was a legal transaction made by Jesus Christ, signed in His blood. And as we'll see in a later session, once we're joined to Christ, nothing can ever separate us from His love.

How does knowing God is a Father help us understand God better?

Abba is a term of endearment like "daddy." What does this title teach us about the particular kind of Father God is to His children?

The Spirit leads us to address God as "Abba, Father!" Abba is only used three times in the New Testament (Mark 14:36; Rom. 8:15; Gal. 4:6) It's an intimate and familiar way of referring to a father. So when Jesus called God *Abba*, He was communicating that God is a particular kind of Father. He's not distant and unknowable. He's close and intimate with us. Jesus eliminated any separation between us and God. We cry "Abba, Father!" because we are God's children.

What does it mean that the Holy Spirit "bears witness with our spirit that we are children of God" (v. 16)? When have you felt this confirmation?

What does a believer being God's child teach us about the love that God has for us?

In verse 16, the first Spirit is capitalized, but the second is not. Paul was referring to the relationship between the Holy Spirit and the internal spirit of a believer. We can call God Father, because the Spirit continually affirms we are His children. This status isn't based on what we have or haven't done. We are fully known, and unconditionally loved. When we follow the Spirit, He reminds us that we are part of God's family, and we have an inheritance in Christ.

Our relationship with God goes beyond being His children—we're also His heirs. What do we stand to inherit from God? Why is our inheritance an affirmation of God's love for us?

Paul referred to believers as "sons" (v. 14). His language was intentional. In the first century, inheritance passed through the male lineage. A father's estate transfered to his firstborn son. Because Jesus is God's Son, everything God has belongs to Jesus. Because we belong to Christ, everything Christ has belongs to us. God has not withheld any of the blessings or privileges of sonship from us. At every moment, we can be assured of God's love for us because of everything He's done to prove it. We are adopted, beloved, children of God.

Pause for a moment and consider all God has done for us. How can you remind yourself of these truths the next time you feel unloved?

Praise God for loving you and adopting you into His family.

REFLECT

This session is all about our fear of being loved. We all have moments in our Christian journey where we feel as though our sin is too much or we've gone too far over a line. We have doubts and desire assurance of God's love for us. The best way to overcome our doubts and fears is to confront them with truth from God's Word.

Below are a few statements that distill the key points from this session. Respond to each one in the space afterward. Do you agree? Where do you have trouble accepting this? Use this space to praise God and pray.

God has adopted you into His family. You are fully known and unconditionally loved by Him.

Because you have been adopted by God, He is your Abba (Father). Nothing you have ever done or ever could do has the ability to change this reality.

The Holy Spirit lives inside of you and testifies to your spirit that you are a child of God. If you learn to listen to Him, He will assure you of your standing before God.

You are a coheir with Christ. Everything that belongs to Christ is yours. All He has been given from God, He gives to you. God loves you in the same way He loves Jesus.

You are no longer an orphan. The spirit of fear that once enslaved you is broken. When you feel unloved or unlovable, those are not trustworthy feelings.

REHEARSE

This session, we're adding a third verse to our memorization passage. How does it feel to be storing God's Word in your heart? Hopefully it's more rewarding than you imagined.

Who shall bring any charge against God's elect? It is God who justifies.
ROMANS 8:33

Begin this week by rereading Romans 8:31-32 several times to refresh your memory. Then read this week's verse, emphasizing a different word each time until you feel comfortable. Try putting the verses on note cards to carry with you and practice when you have a spare moment.

A Scripture memory card for this verse can be found on page 139.

8

ROMANS

FROM BROKEN TO BELONGING

SESSION 4

Suffering

GROUP STUDY

Start

Welcome everyone to session 4.

What was your most significant takeaway from last session about our adoption in Christ?

Has anyone been memorizing the passage in Romans 8? If so, how's that going? What are you learning?

Last session we talked about combating our fear of being loved with the truth of our adoption in Jesus Christ. This week we're going to examine suffering in the life of a believer.

When have you seen something good or helpful come from a truly painful situation?

No one enjoys suffering. Yet, no one can escape suffering. All of us understand that suffering comes in unexpectedly and stays as long as it wants. It never knocks or gives us time to prepare for its grand entry, it just comes. It comes in the middle of a momentous occasion, a celebration, or in the most peaceful time of our lives. No one can ever truly prepare for suffering, but we can prepare to suffer well. That's what this session is all about.

To prepare for video session 4, pray that God will help each person understand and apply this truth:

Knowing God well will help you suffer well.

To access the teaching sessions, use the instructions in the back of your Bible study book.

Watch

*Use the space below to take notes while
you watch video session 4.*

Discuss

*Use the following questions to guide
your discussion of the video.*

Begin by reading Romans 8:18-25 together.

1. Suffering is part of living in a broken world, and we cannot control when suffering comes into our lives. Why does the unexpected nature of suffering make it so difficult to walk through?

2. What are some examples of suffering we have in the Scriptures? How did these men and women suffer well? Which one is most helpful for you?

3. Noe mentioned there are a couple of lies people believe about suffering. First, some believe suffering happens because we've sinned and God is punishing us. While we certainty can suffer because of our sin, why is this often not the case? How might viewing suffering this way harm our relationship with God?

4. The second lie we believe about suffering is that if we're suffering and haven't sinned, God will reward our suffering. How does this lie actually make our suffering more painful?

5. Read Romans 8:18. According to Paul, what was the secret for suffering well? What would it look like for us to embrace this secret in our own sufferings?

6. Read Revelation 21:3-4. What benefits await believers in the future? How do these benefits help us place our suffering in perspective?

7. How can we regularly remind one another about the future benefits while also recognizing the painful reality of present suffering?

8. Who is suffering in our community? What are some tangible ways we can support them and point them to the hope of the gospel?

As you end your time together, remind group members to complete this session's personal study. Then pray together, thanking God that our suffering in this broken world is light and momentary compared to the joy awaiting us in future glory.

READ

Paul was a seasoned sufferer. He was beaten, mocked, imprisoned, shipwrecked, and left for dead all because he was trying to reach the known world with the gospel. Following Jesus intensified Paul's suffering, yet he was able to maintain a perspective that allowed him to suffer well.

As you read the following verses, take note of what Paul wrote about the reality of suffering as well as the certainty of hope. List your observations below.

¹⁸ For I consider that the sufferings of this present time are not worth comparing with the glory that is to be revealed to us. ¹⁹ For the creation waits with eager longing for the revealing of the sons of God. ²⁰ For the creation was subjected to futility, not willingly, but because of him who subjected it, in hope ²¹ that the creation itself will be set free from its bondage to corruption and obtain the freedom of the glory of the children of God. ²² For we know that the whole creation has been groaning together in the pains of childbirth until now. ²³ And not only the creation, but we ourselves, who have the firstfruits of the Spirit, groan inwardly as we wait eagerly for adoption as sons, the redemption of our bodies. ²⁴ For in this hope we were saved. Now hope that is seen is not hope. For who hopes for what he sees? ²⁵ But if we hope for what we do not see, we wait for it with patience.
ROMANS 8:18-25

How did Paul describe the reality of suffering?

What did Paul say about the certainty of our hope?

When you consider these observations together, what does it teach you about the nature of suffering as a child of God?

Where do you see the "groaning" of the world around you? What are some ways the created world reveals it has been broken by sin?

Why should Christians be the first people to acknowledge the groaning and disorder of creation rather than dismissing it?

There's a tendency among Christians to explain away suffering by saying it will all work out, or worse, they might believe that suffering is the result of sinfulness on the part of the sufferer. To be clear, some people do suffer because of personal sin, but that kind of suffering is usually obviously linked to specific sin. More often, suffering happens because the world is broken and decaying. However, all our pain and suffering will eventually give way to glory. Paul used a helpful metaphor to describe this process.

How does the analogy of childbirth help us see our suffering from a different perceptive?

How does this analogy help us see the goodness of God in and through our suffering

Paul used the word *groan* three times in Romans 8 (vv. 22-23, 26). The whole earth is pregnant with labor paints. However, like a woman going through labor pains, our suffering is only momentary and will give way to indescribable joy. Suffering as a child of God is a painful privilege. Suffering is always painful, and that shouldn't be ignored. But it's also a privilege because suffering doesn't have the last word. Our present sufferings have a limited lifespan.

Even though our sufferings are temporary, why should we still mourn them?

Though we mourn, how does our adoption as children of God give us confidence during trials?

Christianity does not give us a free pass out of suffering. And it is good and right to acknowledge the real pain in our suffering. Being a child of God doesn't mean our suffering will be less severe or more endurable. It does mean that we can see our suffering as one point on a timeline that extends into eternity. For the Christian, the best is always ahead of us. That's the hope of this passage.

How might this passage help you minister to a hurting friend or family member?

The real reward for our suffering is what God does in us and through us. There is an intimacy with God that happens amidst our suffering that only suffering can produce. It stabilizes our feet on solid ground and not sinking sand, and our souls are touched by the Creator Himself, who is present with us in our suffering.

> *Pray for your hurting friends and family, asking God to comfort them. Pray that God would help you find hope in your present sufferings as you long for future glory.*

REFLECT

To be a Christian is to enter the school of suffering. To say "yes" to Christ is to say "yes" to suffering. It's allowed by God and sometimes ordained by God. Yes, you read that correctly. God ordains suffering! He did for Jesus and you don't have to look very hard in Scripture to find faithful saints who suffered well. Paul was no stranger to suffering. He saw his incredible suffering as a way to point others to his incomparable Savior.

> [24] Five times I received at the hands of the Jews the forty lashes less one. [25] Three times I was beaten with rods. Once I was stoned. Three times I was shipwrecked; a night and a day I was adrift at sea; [26] on frequent journeys, in danger from rivers, danger from robbers, danger from my own people, danger from Gentiles, danger in the city, danger in the wilderness, danger at sea, danger from false brothers; [27] in toil and hardship, through many a sleepless night, in hunger and thirst, often without food, in cold and exposure. [28] And, apart from other things, there is the daily pressure on me of my anxiety for all the churches. [29] Who is weak, and I am not weak? Who is made to fall, and I am not indignant? [30] If I must boast, I will boast of the things that show my weakness. [31] The God and Father of the Lord Jesus, he who is blessed forever, knows that I am not lying.
>
> 2 CORINTHIANS 11:24-31

Why did Paul brag about his weakness? Why does this seem odd in our culture?

Consider the suffering and adversity you've experienced. List some of the hardships you've faced so far in life.

How did God lead you through that suffering? How did He make Himself known during your suffering?

How could you boast in God as a result of your weakness?

Use the space below to write out your experience with suffering and hope. How has hurt lead you to find hope?

REHEARSE

Hopefully as we work on memorizing Scripture, the truths of Romans 8 are beginning to impress themselves on your soul through the power of the Holy Spirit. This session, we're going to be memorizing verse 34.

Who is to condemn? Christ Jesus is the one who died—more than that, who was raised—who is at the right hand of God, who indeed is interceding for us.

ROMANS 8:34

Begin this week by rereading Romans 8:31-33 to refresh your memory. Then read this week's verse 10 times slowly. As you grow more comfortable, read them together. Use the blank space to write out the verses a few times. Consider reaching out to a friend in your group to see how they're doing and to hold each other accountable.

A Scripture memory card for this verse can be found on page 139.

ROMANS

FROM BROKEN TO BELONGING

SESSION 5

Purpose

GROUP STUDY

Start
Welcome everyone to session 5.

What was your most significant or helpful takeaway from the last session?

Last session, we talked about suffering in our lives. This week we're going to talk about how God turns our pain into purpose.

Have you ever been hurting and had someone tell you, "It will all work out"? Why is that a frustrating sentiment to hear when we're in pain?

Can you imagine living a life where pain has no purpose? A life where all of the hardship has no meaning or value. This would be defeating. What would be the point? This would be like being dropped in the middle of the ocean with no land in sight. It feels pointless to continue swimming. It's hopeless, and you are just waiting to sink. But thankfully, life isn't like that with God. See, because of God, our pain isn't in vain, it has meaning and purpose.

To prepare for video session 5, pray that God will help each person understand and apply this truth:

> God can turn pain into purpose.

 **To access the teaching sessions, use the instructions in the back of your Bible study book.**

Watch

Use the space below to take notes while you watch video session 5.

Discuss

*Use the following questions to guide
your discussion of the video.*

Begin by reading Romans 8:26-30 together.

1. What is the difference between saying "all things are good" and "all things can be used for good"? Why is the distinction important for believers?

2. Romans 8:28 says that we can *know* that God is working all things for our good. What about God's character gives us the confidence to *know* that He's working all things for our good?

3. What circumstances in our lives do we doubt that God could use for good?

4. When going through trying times, it is common to ask questions like "Why did this happen?", "Why did this take place?", or "How does this make sense?" Why are these good questions to take to God? What keeps us from going to God with our pain?

5. Look back at verses 26-27 again. Sometimes, in our pain, we can't find the words to pray. What role does the Holy Spirit play in our prayer lives when we're struggling? How does this reflect God's care and provision for us?

6. What are some ways we can point one another back to God's character when we're hurting? How can we do this while also being sensitive to the genuine hurt our friends are experiencing?

7. Noe ended the teaching session saying, "We are not free from brokenness, but we are free from hopelessness." How does hope give us purpose? Where are you finding hope right now?

As you end your time together, thank God for using all things for your good and His glory. Ask Him to give you patience when you do not understand His will and the wisdom to recognize His heart. Remind group members to complete this session's personal study.

READ

So far in our walk through Romans 8 we've touched on how God has redeemed us, given us life through His Spirit, brought us into His family, and given us hope for a future in the middle of a fallen world. This session we're going to focus on one of the most well-known verses in Romans and see how God takes our pain and uses it for His purpose.

As you read the following verses, underline every promise of God you find. Take notice of how these promises connect to God's purpose for our lives.

26 Likewise the Spirit helps us in our weakness. For we do not know what to pray for as we ought, but the Spirit himself intercedes for us with groanings too deep for words. 27 And he who searches hearts knows what is the mind of the Spirit, because the Spirit intercedes for the saints according to the will of God. 28 And we know that for those who love God all things work together for good, for those who are called according to his purpose. 29 For those whom he foreknew he also predestined to be conformed to the image of his Son, in order that he might be the firstborn among many brothers. 30 And those whom he predestined he also called, and those whom he called he also justified, and those whom he justified he also glorified.
ROMANS 8:26–30

List the promises you underlined below.

Take a closer look at Romans 8:28. What does "all things" mean within the context of that verse?

"All things" in this passage can mean several things. One, all of the sin we face. All of our poor decisions. Another is all the unfortunate things that happen to us. Sometimes we experience pain that comes from living in a sinful world. We didn't do anything to invite the suffering; it just happened. Also included in all things are the pleasant and helpful things that happen to us. Paul was saying that God takes all the pieces of our lives and arranges them for our ultimate good. However, "good" here does not mean earthly good. To understand what Paul meant, we need to consider who this passage is for.

Who is being promised something in verse 28? Why does this distinction matter?

In this passage, God is making a promise. If there is a promise to be claimed, we must know who the promise is for. Paul said that it's *for those who love God, who are called according to His purpose.* This limits the application of God's promise to Christians. That changes what Paul meant by "good." In the context of these verses, it doesn't mean we will get a good doctor's report this week. It doesn't mean we will get that thing we've been hoping and praying for. Scripture determines how we define the word *good.* In the original language of the New Testament, the word *good* can also mean useful. And for the believer, God defines what is good and what is useful for us. Moving further into the passage, Paul further explained the good God is promising.

First, God will conform us into the image of His Son (v. 29). Why do we need to be conformed into the image of Christ?

How did God use Jesus' suffering to bring about our good? How does this help you understand how God can use every part of your experience for good?

We can trust that God is for our good because He's had a plan from before time began. God foreknew (or planned ahead of time) to make us like Jesus. To be conformed into the image of Christ means to become increasingly like the One who broke the power of sin and death. Because Jesus is unstained by sin, He doesn't experience any of the brokenness we experience. At every moment, He experiences perfect fellowship with the Father. In His grace, God takes the broken pieces of our lives and uses them to make us look more like Jesus.

If Jesus is the firstborn among many brothers, what does that teach us about our relationship with God through Christ?

How does the resurrection of Jesus give us hope for the future?

Second, God has given us a future in heaven. The second good requires further explanation. We are being confirmed into the image of Christ who is the firstborn among many brothers (v. 29). In context, we are those brothers. Jesus is both the firstborn of all creation and the firstborn of the dead (Col. 1:15, 18; Heb. 1:6; Rev. 1:5). To be conformed into the image of Christ means that we will be raised from the dead just like Jesus was raised from the dead. In heaven we will be conformed to the image of God—spiritually, morally, and physically.

How does knowing all of our experiences—good, bad, and otherwise—are preparing us for a future in heaven change the way you feel about the circumstances of your life?

The third good God promises in this passage is that we will be glorified. This means that in the future, our bodies will be redeemed and resurrected like Jesus' body was when He rose from the dead. God's plan for us extends from before time began into eternity. Because God has a plan, we can trust that all of the stuff we go through—cancer, death, heartache, and poor decisions—can be taken and used for our good. There is extreme security and comfort in knowing that before we were ever born, God sent His Son to die for us. He loved us from before time began and will love us forever. God collects all of the junk and works it all together, so it has purpose and meaning.

> *Thank God for taking your pain and giving you purpose. Praise Him for His eternal plan to repurpose the broken pieces of your life.*

SESSION 8

Conquer

GROUP STUDY

Start

Welcome everyone to session 8.

Last session we looked at how there is nothing that can ever separate us from Christ. This session, we're going to see how that makes us more than conquerors.

What is your favorite underdog story—it could be from movies, TV, sports, or the news?

When has God given you a win that you never would've gotten on your own?

Victory is much sweeter when it's not handed to you! But there is no better victory story than the story that God writes. When God writes stories of victories in Scripture, they are typically filled with underdogs like Moses, Joshua, Esther, David, and Isaiah—characters who really can't do it on their own. They didn't have enough resources or man power to accomplish the tasks ahead, but by the end they persevered, overcame, and came out with a surpassing victory! The same God who helped them overcome and wrote their victory story is the same God who is still writing stories today.

When have you felt the tension between your freedom in Christ and the struggles of the moment?

To prepare for video session 8, pray that God will help each person understand and apply this truth:

> You are a conqueror in Christ.

 **To access the teaching sessions, use the instructions in the back of your Bible study book.**

Watch

*Use the space below to take notes while
you watch video session 8.*

Discuss

*Use the following questions to guide
your discussion of the video.*

Begin by reading Romans 8:37 together.

1. So far in this study we've seen that we are no longer condemned, we are adopted by God as His children, we have been given life by His Spirit, and we can never be forsaken. How do these truths support what Paul taught in this verse?

2. Romans tells us that we are "more than conquerors." The word *conqueror* means "surpassing victory." How is this idea different from the way we typically live as Christians?

3. The story of David and Goliath ends with David's total domination of Goliath (see 1 Sam. 17:51). How does this story and image help us understand what it means to be a conqueror?

4. Noe explained that our being conquerors means death has lost it's sting and sin has lost its power. How does fighting from victory shape our approach to battling sin?

5. What sin is holding you down and making your feel condemned? What would it look like to embrace Christ's victory over this sin?

6. We are not conquerors because of who we are but because of *whose* we are. What changes about our daily lives when we see ourselves as belonging to God? How can we remind each other of these truths?

7. Because we're conquerors, we are also victors—we can celebrate the work Jesus has done to defeat death and sin. What work of Christ in your life do you want to celebrate?

8. Share the most significant truth you've learned over the last 8 sessions. How has this truth impacted your walk with Jesus?

   As you end your time together, thank God for all He has accomplished over the last 8 sessions. Pray that He would continue His work in and through us. Remind group members to complete this session's personal study.

ROMANS

FROM BROKEN TO BELONGING

Leader Guide

TIPS FOR LEADING A SMALL GROUP

Follow these guidelines to prepare for each group session.

Prayerfully Prepare

REVIEW. Review the weekly material and group questions ahead of time.

PRAY. Be intentional about praying for each person in the group.

Ask the Holy Spirit to work through you and the group discussion as you point to Jesus each week through God's Word.

Minimize Distractions

Create a comfortable environment. If group members are uncomfortable, they'll be distracted and therefore not engaged in the group experience. Plan ahead by considering these details: seating, temperature, lighting, food and drink, and general cleanliness. Do everything in your ability to help people focus on what's most important: connecting with God, with the Bible, and with one another.

Encourage Discussion

A good small-group experience has the following characteristics.

EVERYONE IS INCLUDED. Your goal is to foster a community in which people are welcome just as they are but encouraged to grow spiritually. Always be aware of opportunities to include any people who visit the group and to invite new people to join your group.

EVERYONE PARTICIPATES. Encourage everyone to ask questions, share responses, or read aloud.

NO ONE DOMINATES—NOT EVEN THE LEADER. Be sure that your time speaking as a leader takes up less than half of your time together as a group. Politely guide discussion if anyone dominates.

NOBODY IS RUSHED THROUGH QUESTIONS. Don't feel that a moment of silence is a bad thing. People often need time to think about their responses to questions they've just heard or to gain courage to share what God is stirring in their hearts.

INPUT IS AFFIRMED AND FOLLOWED UP. Make sure you point out something true or helpful in a response. Don't just move on. Build community with follow-up questions, asking how other people have experienced similar things or how a truth has shaped their understanding of God and the Scripture you're studying. People are less likely to speak up if they fear that you don't actually want to hear their answers or that you're looking for only a certain answer.

GOD AND HIS WORD ARE CENTRAL. Opinions and experiences can be helpful, but God has given us the truth. Trust God's Word to be the authority and God's Spirit to work in people's lives. You can't change anyone, but God can. Continually point people to the Word and to active steps of faith.

Keep Connecting

Think of ways to connect with group members during the week. Participation during the group session is always improved when members spend time connecting with one another outside the group sessions. The more people are comfortable with and involved in one another's lives, the more they'll look forward to being together. When people move beyond being friendly to truly being friends who form a community, they come to each session eager to engage instead of merely attending.

Encourage group members with thoughts, commitments, or questions from the session by connecting through these communication channels:

EMAILS

TEXTS

SOCIAL MEDIA

When possible, build deeper friendships by planning or spontaneously inviting group members to join you outside your regularly scheduled group time for activities like these:

MEALS

FUN ACTIVITIES

PROJECTS AROUND YOUR HOME, CHURCH, OR COMMUNITY

Tips for Leading *Romans 8*

Here are some things to consider for leading this study specifically.

CONSIDER WHEN YOU WANT TO WATCH VIDEOS. Every group member with a book will have access to the teaching videos through a unique code printed on the insert in the back of the book. Each session is 8-12 minutes long. You may suggest group members view the video teaching prior to the group meeting, or you could watch the teaching video together as a group.

CONSIDER WHAT TO COMMUNICATE ABOUT PERSONAL STUDIES. Each session has a group element and an individual element which are both intentionally crafted. *Romans 8* works best when members engage both the group and the personal study. As the leader, you will want to encourage people to complete the personal study throughout the week after the group meeting. Consider sending an email to remind and encourage group members during the week.

Additionally, remember that if you complete the personal study, the people in your group will be more willing to complete it as well.

CONSIDER FORMING SCRIPTURE MEMORY GROUPS. The last personal study exercise—Rehearse—guides group members to memorize Romans 8:31-39. This is likely a new spiritual discipline for many people in the group. They may feel overwhelmed. However, Scripture memory is quite easy if we're willing to give it the time. It may be helpful to organize your group into smaller groups for the purpose of memorizing Scripture.

CONSIDER DIFFERENT SPIRITUAL STARTING POINTS. Because of the personal nature of the video teaching coupled with the deep spiritual truths disclosed in Romans 8, you'll want to keep in mind the different spiritual starting points of the group members. Some sessions may include theological ideas that are new or that someone may not have thought through clearly. Maybe that's you. That's okay. Realize we all come from different places and that's okay.

SHAME

KEY TRUTH

Jesus frees you from sin and condemnation.

FOCAL PASSAGE

Romans 8:1-4

MEMORY VERSE

Romans 8:31

CONSIDERATIONS

- You'll want to use this session to introduce both the study and the group members to one another
- Condemnation is a very present feeling for many Christians. Treat this like a real struggle even if you don't experience the feeling yourself.
- This session asks people to share about shame. This might be difficult. Be patient and be willing to share yourself.
- Continue to point people back to the God who loves and accepts them.

NOTES

BATTLEFIELD

KEY TRUTH
Setting your mind on the cross helps you
embrace the Spirit's work in your life.

FOCAL PASSAGE
Romans 8:5-11

MEMORY VERSE
Romans 8:32

CONSIDERATIONS
- We all face spiritual battles of some kind. Our tendency is to hide these from one another. We need to bring these to light to expose them to the gospel.
- Focus on how the group can help one another with their spiritual battles.
- One or more people in your group might be in the middle of a spiritual battle.
- Noe mentions memorizing Scripture as a way to fight spiritual battles. Use this to highlight the Scripture memory focus of this study.

NOTES

....

....

....

....

....

....

....

....

....

PHILOPHOBIA

KEY TRUTH
God loves you.

FOCAL PASSAGE
Romans 8:12-17

MEMORY VERSE
Romans 8:33

CONSIDERATIONS
- Make sure to define *philophobia*—the fear of being loved.
- Press into the teaching on adoption.
- Adoption has three benefits. 1) Our debt is removed 2) We have a new name. 3) We are heirs with Christ.
- Remind the group that being adopted by God is the assurance that we are loved. We may not feel loved, but we are loved at every moment.
- The Holy Spirit is what gives us the spirit of adoption. Many may not have fully considered their relationship to the Holy Spirit.

NOTES

....

....

....

....

....

....

....

....

SUFFERING

KEY TRUTH
Knowing God will help you suffer well.

FOCAL PASSAGE
Romans 8:18-25

MEMORY VERSE
Romans 8:34

CONSIDERATIONS

- The suffering described in this session is suffering that comes from living in a broken world, not the kind of suffering that comes as a result or consequence of personal sin.
- Someone in your group is likely suffering so be aware that this session might be like pulling back a scab for them.
- Suffering with God on our side is still suffering, and it is still painful. Avoid minimizing or dismissing someone's experience.
- Find tangible ways to support those who are suffering in your community.

NOTES

PURPOSE

KEY TRUTH

God can turn pain into purpose.

FOCAL PASSAGE

Romans 8:26-30

MEMORY VERSE

Romans 8:35

CONSIDERATIONS

- "All things work for good" is different than "all things are good." Make sure the group understands this distinction. Many bad things happen to us that are objectively not good. The point is God can ultimately use those things.
- It is okay to be confused or bewildered about the work God is doing through pain. Expect that people have been confused by their experience of suffering.
- Continually point people to the hope and purpose that comes from knowing Christ.

NOTES

....

....

....

....

....

....

....

....

....

TRUST

KEY TRUTH
God is for you.

FOCAL PASSAGE
Romans 8:31-34

MEMORY VERSE
Romans 8:36

CONSIDERATIONS

- Share with the group the reasons that you feel God is trustworthy.
- Draw attention to the fact that bad things will happen to us. Those things are not evidence that God is not for us, but that the world is broken and in need of redemption.
- Focus on how we can help one another trust God in all circumstances. Trust is fostered in community.
- You may have people in your group who have trouble trusting God or others. Point out that Noe experiences the same thing. Make space for this viewpoint.

NOTES

....
....
....
....
....
....
....

SEPARATION ANXIETY

KEY TRUTH

Nothing can separate us from God.

FOCAL PASSAGE

Romans 8:35-39

MEMORY VERSE

Romans 8:37

CONSIDERATIONS

- Point out that nothing can ever separate us from the love of God in Christ. Draw attention to the things that make us feel separated from Christ and point out how Jesus has overcome all of them.
- Note that some people feel separation because they push people away before they can hurt them. Affirm that your group is a place where people can trust and depend upon one another.
- State that we can never out-sin God's love for us. It is fixed and immovable. We can never do anything that will make God stop loving us.

NOTES

....

....

....

....

....

....

....

....